Ferruccio Brugnaro

FIST OF SUN
PUGNO DI SOLE

Translated by Jack Hirschman

CURBSTONE PRESS

Printed in Canada on acid-free paper by Best Book Manufacturers
Cover design: Stone Graphics

This book was published with the support of the
Connecticut Commission on the Arts, the National
Endowment for the Arts, and donations from many
individuals. We are very grateful for this support.

Some of these translations have appeared in the *Anderson Valley Advertiser*, *Arshile*, *Axis*, *Collision*, *Compages*, *Poetry USA* and the *People's Tribune*.

Library of Congress Cataloging-in-Publication Data

    Brugnaro, Ferruccio, 1936-
        [Poems. English. Selections.]
        Fist of sun / by Ferruccio Brugnaro; translated by Jack
    Hirschman.
            p.   cm.
        ISBN 1-880684-52-7
            1. Brugnaro, Ferruccio, 1936-   —Translations into English.
    I. Hirschman, Jack, 1933-   . II. Title.
    PQ4862.R73A25   1997
    851'.914—dc21   97-22945

published by
CURBSTONE PRESS   321 Jackson Street   Willimantic, CT 06226
phone: (860) 423-5110   e-mail: curbston@connix.com
http://www.connix.com/~curbston/

*This translation is dedicated to
Alessandro Spinazzi*

CONTENTS

INTRODUCTION xi

NON DIRE CHE MI SPIEGHI 2
DON'T TELL ME TO EXPLAIN 3

MA IO RESTO UN COMUNISTA 6
BUT I REMAIN A COMMUNIST 7

I COMPAGNI PREDILETTI 8
THE DEAREST COMRADES 9

LA SOLITUDINE, LA FAME LANCINANTE 10
THE LONELINESS, THE PIERCING HUNGER 11

VENTI ANNI DOPO 12
TWENTY YEARS AFTER 13

UN GIORNO O L'ALTRO 14
ONE DAY OR ANOTHER 15

IL NOSTRO GIORNO 16
OUR TIME 17

COMPRA, CONSUMA SEMPRE 18
BUY, ALWAYS CONSUME 19

NON MI VERGOGNO, GRIDATELO DOVUNQUE 20
I'M NOT ASHAMED, SHOUT IT EVERYWHERE 21

BRACCIANTE, RACCOGLITORE DI STRACCI 24
LABORER, RAGPICKER 25

VOGLIO STRINGERTI, STRINGERTI 28
I WANNA HUG YOU, HUG YOU 29

LUIGI E GABRIELE 30
LUIGI AND GABRIELE 31

NON DITEMI DI NON DISTURBARVI 32
DON'T TELL ME NOT TO BOTHER YOU 33

NON VOGLIAMO PIU PADRONI 34
WE DON'T WANT BOSSES, PERIOD 35

NON VEDRA MAI PIU FORSE 36
MAYBE HE'LL NEVER SEE AGAIN 37

DIVERTIMENTO 38
HAVING FUN 39

NON POSSO STACCARMI 42
I CAN'T LEAVE 43

L'ASSEMBLEA DI FABBRICA 44
FACTORY ASSEMBLY 45

VOGLIO DIRE IO ORA 46
I MEAN NOW 47

L'ALTRO GIORNO L'HO SOPRESO 48
I WAS SURPRISED THE OTHER DAY 49

LA FABRICA OGGI 52
TODAY THE FACTORY 53

NELLA NOTTE E ESPLOSO UN REPARTO 54
ON THE NIGHT A SECTION EXPLODED 55

BASTA CON QUESTA ATROCE GUERRA 58
ENOUGH WITH THIS HORRIBLE WAR 59

DOPO UNA NOTTE DI PIOGGIA 60
AFTER A NIGHT OF RAIN 61

IL CORTEO OPERAIO 62
THE WORKER PROCESSION 63

SIAMO ENTRATI NELLE TERRE 64
WE'VE GONE TO THE LAND 65

QUELLI CHE PERDONO SEMPRE   66
THOSE WHO ALWAYS LOSE   67

I CIELI DELL'EROINA   70
HEROIN SKIES   71

DOLCISSIMA E LURID   76
MELLOWEST AND LURID   77

RUFFIANI DELLA GUERRA   78
WAR-PIMPS   79

RAGAZZI DI PALESTINA   80
CHILDREN OF PALESTINE   81

LA VOCE TACE, NON RICEVE VOCE   84
THE VOICE STILLS, DOES NOT RECEIVE VOICE   85

MANIFESTAZIONE OPERAIA   88
WORKERS' DEMO   89

C'È UNA STELLA, MARIA, STASERA   90
THERE'S A STAR, MARIA, THIS EVENING   91

SOLO LA TRIONFA   92
IT ALONE TRIUMPHS   93

NEVE DI PRIMAVERA   94
SPRING SNOW   95

INTRODUCTION

Ferruccio Brugnaro is a poet whose work is governed by an irresistible directness, a hands-on sincerity organized into an agit-prop confrontation expressing a modern classical tradition that's been declared either dead in the water or non-existent in the first place.

Poetry is not supposed to grab you by your lapels or, lacking a coat (as many are these days), your collar.

It's not supposed to stick its verb in your face.

Or come at one as if there were an urgency that needed immediate involvement.

In short, Brugnaro's poetry is poetry, necessary and gritty. Militant. Revolutionary. With a spine of discourse come from real and not imagined discourse: actual participation in actual struggles and not the imagining of or commentaries upon such struggles.

Brugnaro was born in Mestre, Italy, on August 18, 1936. He worked for more than thirty years—most of his adult life—in the giant complex of chemical factories in the Porto Marghera district of Venice. He retired from factory work in 1992 and now devotes all of his time to his writings.

But since 1959, Ferruccio has made poetry and the politics of the worker an integral part of his life. Though numerous books of poems and stories and thoughts are making their way to a wider and wider audience in Italy, he remains (blessedly, thankfully) outside the"literary" and bankrupt tendencies of Italian culture. He is a union guy, close to the street, an agit-propagandist poet, with a mimeo heart in tune and touch with the struggles of the workers and those falling into utter poverty, destitution and, through the cracks, to death.

I first came in contact with his work in the latter part of the '80's, when *Compages*, an international journal of poetry I was helping to edit, published one of his poems.

Then, in January of 1993, when I was on a reading tour throughout Italy, on the occasion of the bi-lingual publication of my own book poems, *Endless Threshold*, I had the great fortune finally to meet Ferruccio—at the home of our mutual friend and comrade, Alessandro Spinazzi.

We all had a great week together in and around the Venice area. Ferruccio and I read one evening at Lenin Hall in the building of the old—now changing—Italian communist party, during a discourse I was giving on the changes demanded in the electronic world vis-a-vis unemployment and robotization.

A few days later, we all drove (including his wife, Maria) to Vittoria Veneto, where Ferruccio and Maria read the Italian of my poems, and I read the original American.

I decided, during that week of happy cameraderie, and because I see in Ferruccio's work a resonance that harks back to Mayakovsky, as well as forward toward the necessary future of mankind, to translate his poems in a selection that might include his rage, his righteousness, his tenderness and, through all, that spine of a lyripolitical discourse so very important for the days ahead.

I made my selection from three of his books: *Dobbiamo Volere (We Must Want To); Il Silenzio Non Regge (The Silence Doesn't Rule),*and *Le Stelle Chiare di Queste Notti (The Clear Stars of These Nights).*

My thanks to Katy Bird and Alessandro Spinazzi in Marghera, Italy, and to Susanna Bonetti and Antonella Soldaini in San Francisco for helping shape the first and second drafts of this translation, respectively; and to Franco Francesca, in Hebden Bridge, England, who went over the text and provided many helpful suggestions as well.

I am certain Americans will recognize more than a little of themselves in the poetry of this wonderful Italian internationalist.

—Jack Hirschman
San Francisco 1997

FIST OF SUN

NON DIRE CHE MI SPIEGHI

Dentro questa notte d'inverno
il mio cuore
in giro per Roma
è una belva scatenata.
Non dire che mi spieghi
quei fagotti umani
distesi per terra sul cemento
sotto cartoni scatoloni
dentro coperte
lacere e sporche.
Non dire che mi spieghi
quelle dita
quei piedi
che sbucano neri dagli stracci
come coltelli.
Le mie vene, le mie ossa, i miei
pensieri ora
sono belve inarrestabili
affamate
Non dire che mi spieghi
quelle giovani donne
attorno ai cessi
distrutte come novantenni.
Non spiegatemi niente
dentro questa aspra pioggia
e questa notte di pietra
le mie mani
sono belve con le zampe
alzate
decise
a tutto

DON'T TELL ME TO EXPLAIN

This winter night
    my heart's
a wild, unleashed beast
    going around Rome.
Don't tell me to explain
    these human bundles
stretched out on the concrete
    under cardboard boxes,
    ragged and filthy
    covers inside.
Don't tell me to explain
    these black fingers
    and feet
sticking out of the tatters
    like knives.
My veins and bones and
    thoughts now
are unstoppable, ravenous
    wild beasts.
    Don't tell me to explain
these young women
    around the out-houses
destroyed like 90 year-olds.
Don't explain me nothin'
    inside this sour rain
    and this night of stone
    my hands
are wild beasts with claws
    completely
    resolutely
    raised up,

sono belve feroci
folli
state lontani.
Quei fagotti umani e la belva
ho davanti
dentro
assetata
cieca
che azzanna
che addenta
furiosa
decisa
nel profondo.

are ferocious mad, wild
beasts-
keep your distance!
Those human bundles and the beast
I have in front of me
inside me
thirsty
blind
who tears with fangs
who bites
furiously
right down
to the core.

MA IO RESTO UN COMUNISTA

Fate bene a non fidarvi
    perché anch'io non mi
        fido più di voi.
Avete rinnegato Marx
            e Lenin
    col pretesto che la storia
        cambia sempre.
Avete infangato le lotte operaie
        di questi duri anni
    col discorso
        delle grandi intese.
Avete imparato i metodi
        dei padroni
più sputtanati della terra.
Avete accantonato i combattenti
        che hanno dato tutto
per un mondo con uomini
        non più in ginocchio,
per un mondo senza più umiliazioni
                libero.
Non ho rancore se ora forse
                tocca a me.
Ma se mai ce ne fosse
            bisogno
io resto un comunista
        si, un comunista senza tessera
ma un compagno comunista sincero, vero.

BUT I REMAIN A COMMUNIST

You do good not to trust
  because I don't have
   faith anymore in you either.
You've rejected Marx
  and Lenin
  under the pretext that history's
   always changing,
You've muddied up the working-class struggle
   of these difficult years
  with pronouncements
    of great savvy
learned the bosses'
  methods
for blood-sucking the land even more.
You've tabled the fighters
  who've given everything
for a world where human beings won't have
   to live on their knees
for a world finally free of
   humiliations.
It's not rancour I have now that it's maybe
    my turn.
But if ever there was a need
   to say it,
I remain a communist
  yes, a communist without a party-card
but a really sincere communist comrade.

I COMPAGNI PREDILETTI

Non rifiutate, non odiate
i rivoluzionari
il loro passo carico di futuro
le loro azioni profonde
come le piogge di primavera.
Non calpestateli, non denigrateli più.
Il mondo, la vita rincantucciati
bruciati dal solforico
dalla libidine
li aspetta, li chiama
con invocazioni forti.
Aprite loro le braccia.
Sono i nuovi cieli, i nuovi mattini.
Amateli amateli
come i compagni più prediletti.

THE DEAREST COMRADES

Don't reject, don't hate
        revolutionaries,
    their step charged with future
        their actions deep
as spring rains.
Don't muzzle or dis them any more.
The world, chickenshit life
        burned by acids,
            by libido,
        waits for them, calls to them
            with strong invocations.
Open your arms to them.
The new skies. The new mornings.
            Love them! Love them
like dearest comrades.

LA SOLITUDINE, LA FAME LANCINANTE

Non mi interessa, non mi interessa
                una poesia
che non entra, che non è parte sanguinante
                delle frustrazioni
delle atroci sofferenze
di milioni e milioni di uomini
        costretti ai silenzio
                chiusi in carcere
                        uccisi.
Non mi interessa
una poesia
di suoni piacevoli
divagazioni, astrazioni di merda.
La solitudine, la fame lancinante
del contadino del sud America
                devo raggiungere.
La lotta creatrice accanita
di tutti gli operai della terra
                devo cogliere sempre meglio
                        in profondità
Nell'isolamento, nel dolore disprezzato
                        dei miei compagni negri
nella loro dura angoscia quotidiana
                        nella loro morte
è piantato il mio cuore, la mia azione tenace.

THE LONELINESS, THE PIERCING HUNGER

I'm not interested, just ain't interested in
        a poetry
that won't get into, isn't a bloody part of
        the frustrations
the horrible sufferings
of millions and millions of people
        driven to silence
            locked up in jails
                murdered.
I'm not interested in
a poetry
of amusingly pretty
sounds, abstractions of shit.
I gotta get with
the loneliness, the piercing hunger
        of the South American peasant.
I gotta bottom-line even more
the furious creative struggle
        of all the world's workers.
In the isolation and despised
        pain of my Black comrades,
in their hard daily stress
        and in their dead
my heart and its hard-core actions
        are planted.

VENTI ANNI DOPO

Non parlatene
lasciate stare.
Non fu avvio di terrore
        e di morte.
Cialtroni
menti ammuffite
fu un tempo sconvolgente
        e meraviglioso.
Milioni e milioni di uomini
        uscirono
da una lunga notte.
Fu un tempo di nascite e di crescite
        grandi.
Mafiosi
infami di turno
non avete niente da ricordare
da dibattere, da celebrare.

TWENTY YEARS AFTER

Don't talk of it;
let it be.
Terror and Death didn't begin
                        there.
Hustlers,
mouldy minds—
it was a convulsing
            and wonderful time.
Millions and millions of people
                    fled
            from a long night.
It was a time of births and great
                            growths.
Mafiosi
thugs on duty—
you got nothing to remember,
debate or celebrate.

UN GIORNO O L'ALTRO

Ho saputo qualche giorno fa
    che in Giappone
        un robot è impazzito
    e ha preso per il collo
        il padrone
      senza tante chiacchiere.
Chissà che anche da noi
    un giorno o l'altro
    dopo tanto e tanto girare
  i robot impazziscano
e facciano le stesse o simili cose.

Non mi restano
    tante speranze ancora
      ma questa
        è una delle poche
    che non voglio
mi venga tolta assolutamente.

ONE DAY OR ANOTHER

A few days ago I found out
    that in Japan
        a robot went crazy
    and grabbed the boss
        by the throat
        without so much as a whisper.
One day or other, with us as well
        maybe after rolling
        around a great while
    the robots will go crazy
and do the same or similar things.
I don't have
    many hopes left
    but this is
        one of the few—
    I absolutely
don't want that ever to happen to me.

IL NOSTRO GIORNO

Il cielo è oscuro
                sconvolto.
Il corpo della terra
        oscilla a uno stretto
            cappio d'acciaio
        senza luce
            e senza voce.
Il nostro sogno grandissimo
    vaga ammutolito e cieco
                attorno
        a un lago di fango
                immenso.
Il nostro giorno ora
            è
        lontano
        lontano.

OUR TIME

The sky's dark,
           turbulent.
The body of the earth
           wobbles on a thin
               loop of steel
       without light
          and voice.
Our greatest dream
           is wandering stunned and blind
              around
        an immense lake
            of mud.
Our time now is
     far
     far
     off.

COMPRA, CONSUMA SEMPRE

Compra, compra più che puoi
consuma, consuma. Chiavatene
            di qualsiasi rapporto.
Schiaccia tutto e tutti
compra sempre, porta a casa
                 più che puoi.
Riempiti, riempiti con avidità.
Non guardare in faccia
              nessuno.
Circondati di alte mura
che non ti raggiunga erba
           o voce umana
affonda, affonda nella merda
            più che puoi.
Sta bene in guardia
compra, porta a casa
            consuma sempre.
Guarda in giro, sta attento
che non ti derubino
        schiaccia
           qualsiasi fiore
              qualsiasi pianta.
Compra compra sempre
         porta a casa
            più che puoi
       consuma consuma
affonda, affonda nella merda
merda merda merda.

BUY, ALWAYS CONSUME

Buy, buy more than you can
consume. Consume. Fuck over
       any relationship.
Step on everything and always
    buy everything up. Carry home
      as much as you can.
Stuff, stuff yourself with greed.
Don't look anybody in
       the eyes.
Surround yourself with high walls
so neither grass nor human
       voices can reach you;
sink, sink into shit as deep
      as you can go.
You must be on your guard;
buy away, carry it home
       always consume.
Look around, make sure
they're not robbing you;
      trample
        any flower
          any plant..
Buy, always buy
      carry home
        more than you can carry;
    consume, consume,
sink, sink into the shit,
shit shit shit.

NON MI VERGOGNO,
GRIDATELO DOVUNQUE

Se lottare perché tutti abbiano
                    una casa
un lavoro più umano
e nessuno subisca più
                crudeli ingiustizie;
se metterci contro la guerra
                    quotidianamente
buttando avanti sempre gli sfruttati;
se incomodare i politici, l'ordine
                costituito, i vescovi
per l'uguaglianza di tutti gli uomini
significa essere estremisti, pazzoidi
                    pericolosi
incapaci, infantili;
ebbene, io allora sono un estremista
                un pazzoide pericoloso
un incapace, un infantile.
Non mi vergogno. Ditelo dovunque.
Ditelo alla Casa Bianca, in Vaticano
                al Cremlino.
Gridatelo nelle piazze, nelle fabbriche.
Non sono mai stato cosi felice.
Voglio essere estremista
             estremista
             estremista fino in fondo.
Si urli questa notizia
in tutti i quartieri, nelle città
su tutte le piazze e le strade della terra.
Gridatelo con forza alle autorità
                alla legalita.

I'M NOT ASHAMED,
SHOUT IT EVERYWHERE

If struggling so that everyone has
                a place to live
a more human job
and no one suffers cruel injustice
                anymore;
if standing up everyday
                against war
and kicking the butts of the exploiters;
if shaking up politicians, the status
                quo and the clergy
in the name of equality for all mankind
means we're extremists, dangerous
                and crazy
and infantile—
well, then, I'm a dangerous
                crazy and infantile
extremist.
No. I'm not ashamed. Spread it everywhere.
Tell the White House, the Vatican
                and the Kremlin as well.
Shout it in the streets and in the factories too.
Never have I been so happy.
I wanna be extremist
                extremist
                extremist to the core.
Howl the news
in every neighborhood, every city
in all parks and streets of the land.
Shout it to the authorities
                and the Law.

Sono un estremista convinto.
Sono estremista, estremista
                    fino in fondo
                        cosciente.
Non voglio più disperazione
                solitudine.
Non voglio più offese che durano
                intere vite.
Voglio sentire giorno per giorno
sempre più vicino, più vicino
i tagli profondi brucianti di milioni
e milloni di uomini che nessuno mai raccoglie.

I'm a confirmed extremist.
I'm extremely extremist
                    conscious to
                        the core.
No more despair and loneliness
                    for me.
No more of those wrong-doings that last
                    a whole lifetime.
Day by day I want to feel
closer, ever closer
to the deep, burning cuts of the millions
and millions of people that no one ever picks up.

BRACCIANTE, RACCOGLITORE DI STRACCI

Bracciante, raccoglitore di stracci
        operaio degli altiforni
           pescatore
      venditore abusivo di crostacei.
    Mio padre
      era cosi
adoratore del sole, adoratore
             delle barene
      silenzioso
      fanatico del mare.
Non ha mai parlato
        con nessuno
      analfabeta
credente solo nella vita
      solo nel suo trascinare
        inquietante
    dai primi cenni dell'alba
      ai tramonti fondi.
    Mio padre
    così come è stato dentro
  in questo mondo torbido
  senza chiedere niente a nessuno
  stanotte è sceso nel tempo
          profondo
nei cieli grandi che lui guardava
      per ore e ore
negli universi incandescenti e amati
      con dura segretezza.
    Non sono triste
    sono felice
      contento

LABORER, RAGPICKER

Laborer, ragpicker
      blast-furnace worker,
         fisherman,
illegal seller of shell-fish—
      that was
      my old man—
a sun-worshipper, a lover
         of shoals
    a silent
      fanatic of the sea.
He didn't talk much
         to anybody,
    was an illiterate
who believed simply in life
   and its disquieting
      thrall
from the first signs of dawn
    to sunset.
That's the way my father
     was inside
   in this murky world
asking nothing from nobody.
Last night he went down to deep
      time,
into the big skies that had watched over him
      hour by hour,
into the incandescent and loving universes,
        with a stiff secrecy.
     I'm not sad
     I'm happy
       content

me lo risento dentro tutto
irruentemente
ora
col suo canto dalla nostra cucina nera
e senza finestre.
Il suo canto, più che un canto
il suo era ed è
un grido, un urlo selvaggio
denso
che io rilancio con tutta
la forza delle ferite
di un amore a brandelli
contro queste ore
di padroni affamati di sangue
di retate
contro le sbarre pesanti dell'emarginazione
contro le foreste di un dolore
e una solitudine senza fine.

hearing him impetuously
    inside everything
            now
with his song from our dark, windowless
                kitchen
his song that was more than a song
            was a
cry, a wild, dense
            howl
that I toss back with all
        the power of the wounds
    of a love in tatters
against those hours when
the bosses were hungry for our blood
            our hauls
against the heavy bars of marginalization
against the forests of a sorrow
and a loneliness without end.

VOGLIO STRINGERTI, STRINGERTI

Il sole, il sole questa mattina
si è attaccato alla mia carne
            rabbiosamente.
    Ho tanto desiderio
        di sentirmi vivo
            tanto.
Voglio stringerti, stringerti.
Molto gelo c'è tra gli uomini
        le lotte sono estenuanti.
    Ma questo sole
        Maria
    questa terra
        che trema rossa
            di gioia
hanno battuto ogni dura lacerazione.
Non sento ora che queste
            braccia calde.
Non cerco che questo amore meraviglioso.

I WANNA HUG YOU, HUG YOU

Sunshine, sunshine this morning's
      stuck furiously to
         my flesh.
   I want so much
         to feel myself
           alive.
I wanna hug you, hug you.
There's so much ice between people,
    the struggles are exhausting.
   But this sunshine
         Maria
    this land
       that trembles red
     with joy
has beaten off every harsh laceration.
I feel nothing now but these
         warm arms.
I seek only this marvelous love.

LUIGI E GABRIELE

Mi fanno impazzire.
Gridano, litigano.
 Non sono mai sazi
non sono mai stanchi.
 A volte li ammazzerei.
Ma sono la vita
 turbolenta
 bella.

Sono la costruzione
 dirompente
 dell' amore
dentro il tempo e il mondo

LUIGI AND GABRIELE

They drive me nuts.
They yell, they argue.
     They're never satisfied
  never get tired.
     At times I could kill 'em.
But they're life
        turbulent
           beautiful.
The fragmentation-
        balm
    of love
in time and in the world.

NON DITEMI DI NON DISTURBARVI

Blocchi giganti di cemento
    grandi intelaiature di ferro
      lunghi tubi
si sono accampati sul mio sangue.
La polvere, il ferro, gli asfalti
mi hanno ricoperto tutta l'anima.
I miei occhi sono appesi
    a densi funghi gialli
      velenosi
che premono di continuo contro il cielo.
Non ditemi di non chiamarvi,
    di non disturbarvi.
Nelle mie carni si sentono solo
    lunghe grida di sirene
    stridori di lamiere
      rumori aspri.
Le ciminiere sono ferite, crateri
    profondl aperti
      sul mio corpo.
Non ditemi di lasciarvi in pace.
La morte si sta accanendo
    contro la vita.
La morte è tutta scoperta.
Non ditemi che non vi interessa.
Non ditemi che non vi interessa.

DON'T TELL ME NOT TO BOTHER YOU

Giant cement blocks
        huge iron scaffoldings
          long pipes
are camped in my blood.
Dust, iron and asphalt
have covered my whole soul.
My eyes are heavy
        with thick, poisonously yellow
            mushroom clouds
pressing directly against the sky.
Don't tell me not to call on you,
        not to bother you.
What I'm hearing in my flesh is
        long siren-wails
      armor-plated shrieks
          cutting noises.
The smoke-stacks are wounds, deep
        craters open
          on my body.
Don't tell me to leave you alone.
Death's working like a dog
         against life.
Death's laid bare.
Don't tell me you're not interested.
Don't tell me you're not interested.

NON VOGLIAMO PIU PADRONI

Non vogliamo piu padroni
    di nessun genere.
Si sono divertiti gia troppo
    col nostro sangue,
hanno gia fatto troppe feste
    con la nostra vita.
Non fateci tante domande.
Guardate le nostre ferite
    le ferite dei contadini
        dei minatori.
Questa pianta va tolta dal mondo
    una volta per sempre.
Non chiedeteci altro. Abbiamo
    deciso fino in fondo.
Non vogliamo più padroni
perché i padroni
    sono tutti uguali
perché la terra la vogliono
    tutta per loro
perché il sole lo vogliono
    tutto per loro
perché rubano, calpestano
    instancabilmente
perché ammazzano, ammazzano
sotto ogni cielo giorno e notte.

WE DON'T WANT BOSSES, PERIOD

We don't want bosses of any kind,
                    period.
They've already splashed around
                    in our blood,
already feasted plenty
                    on our lives.
Stop asking us so many questions.
Look at our injuries
            the damage done to peasants
                    and miners.
We've gotta yank this plant out of the world
                    once and for always.
Don't ask anything else of us. We've really
                    made up our guts.
We don't want bosses
because they're
                    the same as ever:
because they want the land
            all for themselves,
because they want the sun
            all for themselves
because they never stop
            robbing, trampling
and killing, killing
day and night under every kind of sky.

NON VEDRA MAI PIU FORSE

Un mio compagno oggi in fabbrica
    ha perso un occhio
      con uno spruzzo
       di soda caustica.
Non è escluso che resti cieco.
Non vedrà mai più forse
    il cielo e la terra.
Nessuno di noi più
      potrà guardare in volto
      compagni
non vedrà mai più forse alcun giorno.
Nuova solitudine,
nuovo carico di agghiacciante dolore.
Il nostro cuore, tutto il nostro cuore forse
      sarà lanciato via così
          per sempre
dentro uno straccio inzuppato, nero d'olio.

MAYBE HE'LL NEVER SEE AGAIN

A buddy of mine in the factory today
        lost an eye
           when some caustic
           substance got sprayed.
It's possible he could be blind.
He may never again see
           the sky and the land.
None of us can
           look the comrades in the face
           anymore;
he may never again see another day.
So it's new loneliness,
a new load of hair-raising sorrow.
Maybe our heart, our whole heart will be
           likewise tossed away
               forever
inside a soaking rag black with oil.

DIVERTIMENTO

Bocca, boccassa mille volte bocca
ancora bocca
boccona
leccona.
Occhio del padrone
dita del padrone
lineamenti movimenti finezze
attenti
il padrone
ci guarda ci sente ci culla.
Bocca
boccassa
lecca piscio
lecca buchi
di tutte le sorti
di tutti i culloni.
Giornalista
storico
sociologo
quanto è dolce, quanto è impegnativo
lecca lecca
bocca boccassa
la colpa è tutta degli operai
la colpa è tutta
di chi lavora.
Bocca
boccale
che puzza
non offendiamo la vacca
che ride
al di sopra.

HAVING FUN

Mouth, mouth-box a thousand times mouthy
                    and more mouth
                         big-mouth
                         big-lick-mouth.
Eye of the boss
finger of the boss
sophisticated movements features
                    Watch out,
                         the boss
is watching us, listening to us, rocking us.
                    Mouth,
                    mouth-box
                    licks piss,
                    licks holes,
                    all kinds,
               of all the big-assed ones.
          Journalist,
          historian,
          sociologist,
how sweet and how binding,
                    slurp slurp
                    goes the mouth, the mouth-box,
the fault's entirely the workers'
               the fault's with
                    all those who work.
                    Mouth,
                    stinking
                    jug,
we don't offend the cow
               that laughs
               on top.

39

Bocca
baldracca
lecca lecca

sei in svantaggio
vedono i servi, vedono i padroni
non lasciarti rubare
la merda
boccona
chiavattona
tieni duro
sei piu brava di tutte
le bocche
sei più avanti
di tutti i mercati
di tutti i boccali.

            Hooker
            mouth
        lick lick

                you're at a disadvantage,
the slaves see, the bosses see,
don't let them rob you
                        even your shit
                slut
                mouthful
                        hold on,
            you're better than all
                        the suckers,
                you're way ahead
            of all the markets
            and all the mugs.

NON POSSO STACCARMI

Mi trascino lungo le mura
                    delle fabbriche
giorno e notte.
Sono sempre lungo
                    queste mura.
Non sono capace
non posso allontanarmi.
Molti compagni ho là dentro
            soli in mezzo al fosgene
            davanti a bocche
                    tremende.
Non posso staccarmi.
Il mio cuore ho là dentro
            la mia lotta
                    che arde alta
come una torcia verso il futuro.

I CAN'T LEAVE

I drag myself along factory
                walls
day and night.
I'm always near
                these walls.
Ain't able to,
can't break away.
I got my buddies in there
                alone in the midst of toxics
                    in front of horrible
                        stoke-holes.
I just can't detach.
My heart's inside there,
            my struggle
                burning high
as a torch toward the future.

L'ASSEMBLEA DI FABBRICA

Il sole tossisce rosso in volto
tra nubi dense di anidride solforosa
      pulviscoli giallastri
         terribili.
L'assemblea davanti i cancelli
    è immensa.
Il cielo e la terra testimoniano
        felici.
É tutta un grido preciso
    inconfondibile.
Non vogliamo maschere antigas
nè a Porto Marghera nè altrove.
Impacchettate tutte le vostre fabbriche
       il vostro progresso.
Non vogliamo la morte.
Portate via la morte immediatamente.

FACTORY ASSEMBLY

The sun's coughing red in the face
between dense sulphurous anhydride clouds
              and horrible yellowish
                     hazes.
The demonstration at the gate
           is packed.
Sky and earth are testifying
               happily.
It's all one precise unmistakable
               shout:
We don't want gasmasks,
not here in Porto Marghera, or anywhere else!
Pack up all your factories,
           your progress.
We don't want death.
Get that sucker outta here right now!

VOGLIO DIRE IO ORA

La fabbrica oggi si presenta
                lucida, pulita.
Rose tutto intorno la palazzina
                della direzione.
Rettangoli d'erba ai vari ingressi.
Vicino ai cancelli
qualche pezzo di siepe
                qualche alberello.
Questo è tutto ciò che si vede
ma non è la fabbrica, i reparti
                è tutto ciò che sta sopra.
Voglio dire io ora
                quello che è segreto, che sta nascosto
                                che nessuno dice.
Voglio dire io ora ciò
                che nessun cuore
                                nessuna pietà
                                                raggiunge mai.
Qualcuno di noi ogni giorno.
                viene condotto via
                                in silenzio
con le membra che non reggono più.
Ogni giorno in grande silenzio
                qualcuno di noi
                                si trova
                con i polmoni bucati
                                il cuore rotto.
Molti miei compagni ogni giorno
                senza rumore, senza dolore
in grande solitudine
in grande abbandono se ne vanno via per sempre.

I MEAN NOW

The factory today appears
      shiney, clean.
Roses all around the little
      administration building.
Rectangles of grass at different entrances.
Near the railings
a bit of hedge,
      a few small trees.
That's all one sees;
but that's not the factory, the units,
      all that's above.
What I mean is,
      it's secret, it's hidden away
            and no one talks about it.
What I mean is,
      that's where no heart,
          no pity
            ever gets to.
Every day one of us
      comes down, led away
         in silence
with limbs that don't work anymore.
Every day in that huge silence
      one of us
        is found
    with pierced lungs
      and busted ticker.
Many of my buddies every day
      quietly, contritely,
in great loneliness
and great abandonment, go away forever.

L'ALTRO GIORNO L'HO SORPRESO

Romano Mezzacasa è un compagno
        meccanico
            straordinario .
          Viene dai monti.
Lavora il ferro e l'acciaio
       con una passione
          che non ha eguali.
É duro duro
     come le rocce
       delle sue Dolomiti.
Quando parla della prima neve
      dei caprioli
          che pascolano
             guardinghi
        delle primavere
    bisogna sentirlo
c'è l'amore e il cuore
      di tutto l'uomo.
L'altro giorno l'ho sorpreso
      che stava costruendo
          una trappola
             per topi
    alzò la testa
    e mi disse solo due parole
            decise
ci sono tanti topi in giro
      Ferruccio
         topi schifosi

I WAS SURPRISED THE OTHER DAY

Romano Mezzacasa's an extraordinary
                    mechanic and
                              comrade.
          Comes from the hills.
Works with iron and steel
          with a passion
          that can't be beat.
He's hard, hard
          like the rocks
          of his Dolomites.
When he talks about the first snow,
                    about the does
                              that warily
                                   graze,
               about springtimes,
          you gotta listen to him;
he's got the heart-felt love
               all men do.
I was surprised the other day
                    seeing him building
               a rat-
                    trap;
          he lifted his head
          and said just two determined
                    words to me:
Disgusting rats,
          Ferruccio,
               there are so many running
                         around

ma li prenderemo tutti
      vedrai vedrai
  li prenderemo
     tutti
     tutti.

but we're gonna get 'em all,
        you'll see, you'll see
we're gonna get 'em
      all,
      all.

LA FABBRICA OGGI

La fabbrica oggi stretta in una morsa
                    di gelo
sembra quasi un quartiere abbandonato.
Ghiaccio dappertutto.
Muri, tubazioni,reparti
        ricoperti, bianchi di ghiaccio.
        Grossi chiodi di ghiaccio
    trapassano ora da parte a parte
            le nostre mani, i nostri piedi
                tutto il nostro corpo.
Questa mattina siamo stati
                traditi anche dal sole
che in grande silenzio, in grande segreto
ci aveva rassicurati
                    per un momento
della sua calda, prepotente presenza.

TODAY THE FACTORY

Today the factory's clenched in a vise
                      of frost
and seems like an abandoned district.
Everywhere ice.
Walls, pipes, whole areas
          covered and icy-white.
          Thick spikes of ice
                are piercing our hands,
                      our feet, our whole bodies now.
We've even been betrayed
                      this morning by the sun.
In its great silence, its great secret heart,
it had assured us
                      for a moment
of its warm, forceful presence.

NELLA NOTTE E ESPLOSO UN REPARTO

Fuoco violaceo dappertutto, fumo
          polveri a grandi nuvoloni.
È esploso
     in piena notte
     un reparto chimico.
Si è alzato come un fungo atomico.
Non so quanti miei compagni
                    operai
               siano stati
                    soffocati
               bruciacchiati.
La città è angosciata
     colpita più che da mille
                         bombe,
               atterrita.
La gente è tutta
          un grido
                    lungo
che graffia ogni pietra
               che graffia
                    ogni albero
che morde forte la terra
               e il cielo,
un grido lungo
                    continuato.
     Ascoltiamo, ascoltiamo.
La gente grida tutta
          il popolo
     è tutto un grido
          senza distinzione

ON THE NIGHT A SECTION EXPLODED

Violet flames everywhere, smoke,
        huge dust-clouds.
   A chemical unit's
        blown up
        in the thick of night.
Atomic mushroom-like.
I don't know how many buddies
                workers
         have been
             suffocated
        burned out.
The city's anguished
       struck more than by a thousand
            bombs
         terrified.
The people are all
       one long
         cry
that's clawing every stone
         every
           tree
biting into earth
       and sky
a continuous scream.
      We're listening, listening.
All the people are wailing,
        the people
     all are a single scream
       without distinction

un grido che afferra per la gola
        questa notte d'inferno
                e questo tempo
un grido che è tutto un'alba.

a scream that's grabbing you by the throat
        this hell of a night
            and time
a scream that's all dawn.

BASTA CON QUESTA ATROCE GUERRA

Basta con gli enfisemi polmonari
con le intossicazioni
con le distruzioni sistematiche
silenziose.
Basta con questa atroce guerra
condotta nelle fabbriche
con affermazioni di umanità
di progresso, di amore.
Basta. Il nostro sangue
non ne può più.
Abbiamo abbandonato cabine, centrali.
Abbiamo abbandonato tutti i reparti.
Abbiamo colpito a fondo oggi.
Vogliamo colpire a fondo.
Sotto un sole mai visto prima
ora a migliaia e migliaia
attorniamo la vita.
La vita oggi con tutta la forza
delle nostre ferite
delle nostre angosce
sta premendo decisa
sulla morte il suo piede di fuoco.

ENOUGH WITH THIS HORRIBLE WAR

Enough with these emphysemas
               and poisonings
and systematic, silent
                  destructions.
Enough with this horrible war
           conducted in the factories
          with affirmations of humanity
            progress and love.
Enough. Our blood's
           fed up.
We've abandoned the switchboards, our stations.
We've abandoned all our units.
                Today we've hit hard.
                We wanna hit hard.
Under a sun not seen before
            thousands and thousands of us now
                  are surrounding life.
With the full force
               of our wounds
               and our anguish
          life's decided that today it's putting
its foot of fire down on Death.

DOPO UNA NOTTE DI PIOGGIA

Il mattino e limpido, fresco.
Le ciminiere sembrano lontane.
                Sembra caduto
ogni muro, ogni rete metallica.
                C'è anche
qualche fiore lucido
                nel pugno di terra martoriato
                                che ancora è rimasto.
La nostra carne, il nostro cuore
ora ritornano a essere
                quel sogno guerrigliero
di uccelli e cieli inimmaginabili.

AFTER A NIGHT OF RAIN

The morning's crystal clear.
The smoke-stacks seem far away.
                Every wall,
every wire-mesh seems fallen.
                There's even
some lucid flower
                        leftover in
                the fist of tormented earth.
Our flesh, our hearts
can return now to being
                that partisan dream
of birds and unimaginable skies.

IL CORTEO OPERAIO

Il corteo operaio ora è entrato
        in città
            vociante
come un grande vento.
Le antenne, le piazze, le pietre
sono calde, agitate
        come in primavera.
Stiamo attraversando in questo momento
      il quartiere nobile, pulito
con le sue pezzette d'erba, i suoi alberelli.
Nessuno alle finestre, sui poggioli.
Si sente solo un rumore
        di persiane che si chiudono
          in grande fretta.
Venite, venite fuori
        esplode improvviso il nostro cuore
          in un grido immenso.
Non vogliamo uccidere nessuno,
non vogliamo sfruttare nessuno,
non vogliamo rubare niente a nessuno.
Vogliamo liberare la terra
        da una terra piena di avvilimenti
          massacri calcolati.
Vogliamo portare
un'anima nuova nell'anima del mondo.

THE WORKER PROCESSION

The procession of workers is entering
           the city now
             howling
like a big wind.
The antennae, the streets, the stones
are heating up stirred up
          as in springtime.
At this very moment we're passing through
         the rich neighborhood, clean
with its clipped grass and small trees.
No one's at the windows or on the balconies.
The only sounds
           are slatted shutters closing
             in a big hurry.
Come on out! Come on outside!
              our heart suddenly explodes
                in a vast shout.
We don't want to kill anybody,
don't want to exploit anybody,
don't want to rob anything from anybody.
We want to free the land
          from an earth full of degrading
            calculated massacres.
We want to bring
new soul to the life of the world.

SIAMO ENTRATI NELLE TERRE

Siamo partiti dalle fabbriche
con i disoccupati in 4-5 mila.
L'asfalto sotto i nostri piedi
            sotto il nostro rumore
      freme intensamente.
Il vento scoperchia gli alberi
            e li riempie di sole
      e li fa verdi
            come non mai,
anche i casermoni dei palazzi
                  dove abitiamo
      sono belli
            pieni di vita.
      Entriamo nelle terre
            da occupare
      cantando
      sbraitando
            felici.
Cominciamo a lavorare sodo
                  con vanghe e trattori
scaviamo fossi e tagliamo alberi.
Ma poi il partito e il sindacato
                  dicono
che non c'è niente da fare.
Non bisogna scontrarci.
Non bisogna rompere certi equilibri.
Non bisogna urtare troppo i padroni.
Non capiamo, non comprendiamo.
Non ci convincerete mai
di non batterci, di subire
                  di tacere.
Nessun partito, nessun sindacato
ci convincerà mai di tornare indietro.

WE'VE GONE TO THE LAND

We've left the factories
with the four/five thousand laid off.
The asphalt under our feet
             under our noise
         is quivering intensely.
The wind's sweeping through the trees
             filling them with sunlight
         making them green
             as never before
and the barracks of the buildings
                     where we live
             are beautiful
                 full of life.
     We're going to the land
             to occupy it
             singing
             shouting
             happy.
We begin working with shovels
             and tractors, solidly
digging ditches and cutting down trees.
But then the party and the union
                 say
that there's nothing to be done.
There's no need for a confrontation.
Or for upsetting certain balances.
Or for bumping up against the bosses.
We don't understand, we don't comprehend.
You'll never convince us
to stop fighting, to suffer
                     in silence.
No party, no union
will ever convince us to turn back.

QUELLI CHE PERDONO SEMPRE

Quelli che hanno sempre perso
    in ogni età della terra
    e in ogni stagione
    sono
    le mie carni
    le mie ansie
    i miei stupori.
Quelli che hanno perso
    e perdono
    in tutti i tempi
    hanno i miei stessi passi
    irrevocabili
    il mio duro sguardo
    la mia solitudine.
Quelli che perdono stritolati
    da inesistenti e furbe
                    verità
    dentro eterne carceri
e interminabili inverni
                    sono
    le mie ossa
    la mia arma di opposizione
    il mio dito bruciante
            puntato
    inchiodato
            sulla morte.
Con questi io sono nato
            e sono sempre vissuto
            e vivo
    con quelli che perdono
            sempre
con quelli che perdono

THOSE WHO ALWAYS LOSE

Those who've always, in every
            epoch of the earth,
            in every season,
                lost,
            are my flesh
            my longings
            my amazements.
Those who've lost
                and in every period
                are losing
        irrevocably possess
            my very steps
        my tough look
                my loneliness.
Those who lose, crushed
            by non-existence and cunning
                        truth
                inside eternal jails
        and endless winters
                        are
            my bones
            my arm of opposition
            my burning finger
                    pointed at,
                        nailed
                            to, Death.
I was born with them
            have always lived
                and live
        with them who always
                lose
        with them who go on evermore

sempre di più
che sono trascinati
a perdere con terrore
che pagano tutto
che spendono tutto.
Con questi sono cresciuto
e intendo restare
perché esploda
presto
la luce
che non si piega
che non si inginocchia più
perché salti definitivamente
il gelo
di ogni buio angolo
di ogni dolore
ogni guerra
perché
si apra presto un'altra veduta
del cielo
perché
si vuoti questo mondo
di tanta acredine
perché si aprano
pianeti dolci
stelle dolci
perché si aprano
finalmente
i giorni
i nostri giorni
la terra vera
le nostre strade calde
interminabili .

losing
who are dragged
to lose by terror
        who pay for everything
            who spend everything.
I've grown up with,
            and intend to stick by, them
        because the light
                that's not bowing
        and is no longer down on its knees
                        is about
                    to explode;
because the cold
            from every dark corner,
                        every sorrow,
                            every war
        is definitely going to explode;
                because
another view of the sky is set
                        to unfold
            because
        this world of
                so much acrimony
            is emptying out,
        because gentle planets
            and sweet stars
                are being disclosed
    along with, finally,
            the days that are
                our days
            the real earth
our endlessly warm
                    streets.

I CIELI DELL'EROINA

Il cielo è tutto arancione
e poi verde
e poi bianco
e bello
come la neve
e poi grande
da tutte le parti
nelle vene
su tutta la carne
scende una terra fine
tenera
dolce
dolce
il mondo mi abbraccia stretto
si muove tutto
dentro
solo per me
verso di me
lo afferro
lo afferro
febbricitante.
Sono un petalo incandescente
in una mattina di primavera
spicco il volo
da tutti gli alberi
su tutti i rami
i sogni più ardenti
più amati
mi riempiono le mani
gli occhi
scendo
scendo.

HEROIN SKIES

The sky's all orange
              then green
                then white,
                      and beautiful
              as snow
          and then vast
on every side
              in my veins
      allover my skin
a fine, tender, sweet
                    sweet
          earth
      is descending.
The world hugs me tightly,
          everything stirs
                        within
              only for me
      toward me
              I grab at it
                  I grab at it
                      feverishly.
I'm an incandescant petal
          on a spring morning
          I start flying
from all the trees;
          on all the branches
      the most impassioned, most
              loving dreams
      fill my hands
                  my eyes;
          I descend,
          I descend.

Un sussulto di ghiaccio
             improvviso
una sbarra arrugginita
          macchiata di sangue
             in un'ansa immensa
    uno spillo velenoso
             tetro
    penetra le ossa
       una a una
          terribile
             terribile
il corpo, le carni ammutoliscono
       crollano
          in tristi sudori
       sparisce il fuoco robusto
          delle azalee
             e delle rose
             freddo
                   solitudine
                      gelo
i giardini, i prati
       sono caduti
          in buche
             profonde
       paura
       silenzio
le acque sono torbide
                torbide
       le aurore piangono
    in un dolore
          irreparabile
    cenere
    cenere
il deserto il deserto

A startle of ice
          all of a sudden
a rusted, bloodstained
                    bolt
     in a wide loop,
      a grim, poisonous
                    pin
     penetrates the bones,
          one by one
               terribly
                    awfully.
Body and flesh become mute,
          collapse into
                    sad sweating;
          the robust fire of the azaleas
               and roses
                    disappears;
                    cold,
                         loneliness
                              ice—
The gardens and meadows
               are fallen
                    into deep
                         pits;
          fear,
          silence,
the murky, murky
                    waters;
     the dawns weeping
with irreparable
                    pain:
          ashes
          ashes
the desert, the desert,

cenere
cenere
le mani, la fronte, le viscere
         stordite annebbiate
    sudori dilaceranti
    tremori del nulla
         angoscia
    il nulla
    il nulla
    in bocca alla morte
    in bocca alla morte.

          ashes
          ashes
hands, brows, hearts
               stunned, fogged over,
               agonizing sweating
               shudders of Nothing
                         anguish
          Nothing
          Nothing
     in the mouth unto Death,
     in the mouth unto Death.

DOLCISSIMA E LURIDA

Montagne di chiacchiere.
Oceani di chiacchiere.
Maria
Roma è dolcissima
ma è sporca
            lurida
                  sporca.
Qua si piscia
            in bocca
            al popolo
e si sorride con sarcasmo
            in vaticano, nei ministeri
si vive tranquillamente.

VERY SWEET AND LURID

Mountains of gossip.
Oceans of prattle.
Maria,
Rome is sweet
but it's dirty
        lurid
                filthy.
Here one pisses
        in the mouth
        of the People
and sarcastically smiles
        in the Vatican, in the ministries,
living discreetly.

RUFFIANI DELLA GUERRA

Il fungo intanto sale.
La morte intanto alza
      la voce
         pesante
            schiacciante.
Il vostro amore non l'ho visto.
Bisogna opporsi, opporsi
         mattina e sera.
Il vostro amore non lo sento.
Bisogna esserci esserci
         con tutta la carne
          e con tutta
            la vita.
Ruffiani della guerra.
Ruffiani della morte.
La vostra pace mi terrorizza
la vostra pace è bugiarda
         e ladra
     la vostra pace divora
        anche la notte
la vostra pace
non la voglio, non la voglio.

WAR-PIMPS

Meanwhile the mushroom rises.
And Death meanwhile lifts
               its heavy
                 crushing
                   voice.
I haven't seen your love.
Night and day one has
         to oppose, to be against.
I don't feel your love.
It's gotta be there
              with all your flesh,
                and with your whole
                   life.
Pimps of war.
Pimps of Death.
Your peace terrorizes me,
your peace is liar
          and thief;
       your peace gobbles up
            the night as well.
I don't want
your peace, I don't want it.

RAGAZZI DI PALESTINA

La barbarie cala sul mondo
          spegnendo
     ogni filo di pietà.
La barbarie scorrazza
          da una terra all'altra
     abbattendo anche il più
                    caparbio
                    cenno di vita.
Ragazzi di Palestina
          le vostre fionde
          le vostre pietre
     vengono proprio giuste.
Il cuore umano ora è imprigionato
          tra atroci marmi
il sangue è amalgamato
          muto
          in un turpe vento.
Ragazzi, ragazzi cari
le vostre braccia alzate, il lancio
                    dei vostri sassi
          sono semi ineguagliabili
                    piantati
          sulle pianure, le alture
                    aride antiche
                    del violento
                    e dello sfruttatore.
Non smettete, per carità,
ragazzi ragazzi di Palestina
lanciate, lanciate.
          Le vostre forti grida
               senza ombre

CHILDREN OF PALESTINE

The barbarian strikes at the world
                stifling
        every thread of pity.
The barbarian wanders
                from one land to another
        demolishing the most stubborn
                signs of life
                        as well.
Children of Palestine,
                your slings
                        and stones
                come at the right time.
The human heart now is imprisoned
                by horrible marble;
blood is mixed,
        silent,
        in an ugly air.
Children, dear children,
your raised arms, the hurl
                of your stones
        are seeds unevenly
                planted
on the old arid plains
                and heights
        of the violent
        and the exploiter.
Don't stop, please,
children, children of Palestine,
sling on, sling on.
                Your strong shouts
                        without shadows

le vostre pietre taglienti
in faccia allo sterminatore
sono l'unico profondo amore
che si sente ancora su questa terra.

your stones cutting
into the face of the exterminator
are the deep unified love
one is still able to feel on this earth.

LA VOCE TACE, NON RICEVE VOCE

A Silvano

Nessuno, più nessuno al mondo
crede nel fiore
nel sasso
in te
negli abbisi caldi
e popolati
Il vento ha trasfigurato
ogni stella
ogni voce
la fede più grande
dorme tranquilla
in un letto di fango.
Nessuno crede più di rovesciare
il masso
che schiaccia l'erba
e il dolce insetto.
La voce tace, non riceve voce.
Disordine, sovversione, veleno.
È l'ora del silenzio
del ritiro più assoluto
è l'ora che passa la morte.
Le gemme che bucano
la neve
ora bucano anche il tuo sangue
la tua mente
tu credi, si, credi
resisti
continui.
E chiaro, chiaro
si rovescia su di te ora

THE VOICE STILLS, DOES NOT RECEIVE VOICE

For Silvano

No one, no one in the world
          believes in flowers
              in rocks
              in you
          in warm and populated
              depths anymore.
The wind's transfigured
              every star
          every voice,
          the greatest faith
              is sleeping away
          in a bed of mud.
No one believes anymore in
              overturning the boulder
          that's trampling the grass
          and the sweet insect.
The voice is stilled, does not receive.
Disorder, subversion, poison.
          It's the time of silence
        and the most absolute withdrawal,
          it's the time death is passing through.
        The buds piercing through
              the snow
now also are piercing through your blood
              and your mind.
You do believe, yes, believe,
             resist,
           continue.
It's clear, clear:
        the whole desert

tutto il deserto
ti rovesci sul deserto ora
solo
completamente solo
con sfide possenti
nella carne
incalcolabili.

is spilling on you now,
and you alone,
completely alone, are now pouring
onto the desert
with the powerful defiance
of incalculable
flesh.

MANIFESTAZIONE OPERAIA

Abbiamo stretto Venezia oggi
    in ogni suo angolo.
Striscioni di fuoco alti, slogan
    contro lo sfruttamento, la morte.
Canti di lotta, d'amore ora
    sorgono prepotenti
dal sangue, dall'anima.
Le pietre, le acque sono diventate
    umane, calde.
Il nostro cuore
    corre pazzo
    alla liberazione.
La gioia è immensa.
La vita oggi alza decisa
    nel suo pugno di sole
l'avvenire concreto
degli uomini, di tutti gli uomini.

WORKERS' DEMO

We've gotten hold of
        every corner of Venice today.
Tall red banners, slogans
        against rip-offs and Death.
Urgent songs of
        struggle and love now rise up
from blood and soul.
The stones and the waters have become
        human, warm.
Our heart
        runs madly
          to liberation.
      Huge joy.
Today life raises
        the concrete future
of men, of all mankind,
        in its fist of sun.

C'È UNA STELLA, MARIA, STASERA

C'è una stella
        Maria
     stasera
così limpida e grande
come la lotta che gli sfruttati
stanno sostenendo
       ora nel mondo.
È cosi aggressiva e penetrante
        che mi toglie
           ogni coraggio di parola.
     È come il tuo cuore
       Maria.
È bella
come la terra che stiamo costruendo.

THERE'S A STAR, MARIA, THIS EVENING

There's a star
        Maria
     this evening
so big and clear
like the struggle the poor
are waging
         world-wide now
so up-front and penetrating
       it frees me for
           every courage of the word
     like your heart
        Maria
beautiful as the earth we're constructing.

SOLO LA TRIONFA

Il cielo gocciola sul mare
    un azzurro
      che nessuno
        nessuno
    ha mai conosciuto.
La festa di luce oggi
      ha raggiunto
        ogni dimensione
          ogni cima
            ogni profondità.
    È tutto chiaro ora.
Solo la gioia trionfa
      tra questi scontri
        di rocce e acque
      tra questi dolorosi
congiungimenti di sangue
         e strade.
    È tutto chiaro.
    Solo l'amore trionfa.
Non c'è morte
nelle nostre carni, non c'è morte.

IT ALONE TRIUMPHS

The sky drips a blue
      on the sea
            that no one
      no one
has ever understood.
The feast of light today
      has touched
            every dimension
                  every summit
                        every depth.
   It's all clear now.
Only happiness triumphs
      among these collisions
            of rocks and waters
      among these painful
conjunctions of blood
      and streets.
            Everything's clear.
      Love alone triumphs.
There's no Death
in our flesh, there is no Death.

NEVE DI PRIMAVERA

È sconvolgente
  e bella
  come i tuoi baci
quando sei arrabbiata.
   Scioglie ora
i grovigli di dolore
     più oscuri
in luce intensa e dolce.

Il suo candido morso
     alla terra
  è il tuo morso
  rabbrividente e felice
   alla mia vita
nel cuore della notte.

SPRING SNOW

It's disturbing
  and beautiful
   like your kisses
when you get angry.
   Now the darkest
snarls of pain
    dissolve
into intense, sweet light.
Its pure bite
   at the earth
  is your happy
   shivering nip
    at my life
in the heart of night.

FERRUCCIO BRUGNARO
was born in Mestre, Italy in 1936. He worked for
more than 30 years — most of his adult life — in
the giant complex of chemical factories in the Porto
Marghera district of Venice. He is well-known as a
worker-poet who for years distributed his poems at
the factory he worked at, as well as schools, in
mimeo form — works which now are widely
published. Recently retired, he now devotes full
time to his writing.

JACK HIRSCHMAN
was born in New York City in 1933 and has lived
since 1973 in San Francisco. A poet and translator,
he has published more than 25 translations of
poetry from eight languages, as well as several
volumes of his own poetry including *Lyripol*, *The
Bottom Line* and *Endless Threshold*. He currently
assists in the editing of *Left Curve* and is a
correspondent for *The People's Tribune*.

CURBSTONE PRESS, INC.

is a non-profit publishing house dedicated to literature that reflects a commitment to social change, with an emphasis on contemporary writing from Latin America and Latino communities in the United States. Curbstone presents writers who give voice to the unheard in a language that goes beyond denunciation to celebrate, honor and teach. Curbstone builds bridges between its writers and the public – from inner-city to rural areas, colleges to community centers, children to adults. Curbstone seeks out the highest aesthetic expression of the dedication to human rights and intercultural understanding: poetry, testimonies, novels, stories, children's books.

This mission requires more than just producing books. It requires ensuring that as many people as possible know about these books and read them. To achieve this, a large portion of Curbstone's schedule is dedicated to arranging tours and programs for its authors, working with public school and university teachers to enrich curricula, reaching out to underserved audiences by donating books and conducting readings and community programs, and promoting discussion in the media. It is only through these combined efforts that literature can truly make a difference.

Curbstone Press, like all non-profit presses, depends on the support of individuals, foundations, and government agencies to bring you, the reader, works of literary merit and social significance which might not find a place in profit-driven publishing channels, and to bring the authors and their literature into communities across the country. Our sincere thanks to the many individuals who support this endeavor and to the following organizations, foundations and government agencies: ADCO Foundation, Connecticut Commission on the Arts, Connecticut Arts Endowment Fund, Lawson Valentine Foundation, LEF Foundation, Lila Wallace-Reader's Digest Fund, Andrew W. Mellon Foundation, National Endowment for the Arts, the Open Society Institute, Puffin Foundation, Samuel Rubin Foundation and the Witter Bynner Foundation for Poetry.

Please support Curbstone's efforts to present the diverse voices and views that make our culture richer. Tax-deductible donations can be made by check or credit card to Curbstone Press, 321 Jackson Street, Willimantic, CT 06226, ph: (860) 423-5110, fax: (860) 423-9242.